Legends of SANTA CLAUS

H. Paul Jeffers

Lerner Publications Company
Minneapolis

To Scotty Gordon

A&E and **BIOGRAPHY** are trademarks of the A&E Television Networks, registered in the United States and other countries.

Some of the people profiled in this series have also been featured in A&E's acclaimed BIOGRAPHY series, which is available on videocassette from A&E Home Video. Call 1-800-423-1212 to order.

Lerner Publications Company
A division of Lerner Publishing Group
241 First Avenue North
Minneapolis, MN 55401 U.S.A.

Website address: www.lernerbooks.com

Library of Congress Cataloging-in-Publication Data

Jeffers, H. Paul (Harry Paul), 1934–
    Santa Claus / by H. Paul Jeffers.
      p. cm. — (A&E biography)
    Includes bibliographical references, and index.
    Summary: Relates the story of Santa Claus from his historic origins to his current incarnation, discussing Saint Nicholas, the Americanizing of Santa, his commercialization, and his treatment in songs and movies.
    ISBN 0–8225–4983–2 (lib. bdg.)
    1. Santa Claus—Juvenile literature. [1. Santa Claus.] I. Title.
II. Series.
GT4992.J43   2001
394.2663—dc21
    [B]   99–27240

Manufactured in the United States of America
1 2 3 4 5 6 – JR – 06 05 04 03 02 01

CONTENTS

Gliding quietly through the sky, Santa and his reindeer are sometimes humorously classified as unidentified flying objects by government agencies.

INTRODUCTION

THE NORTH AMERICAN AEROSPACE DEFENSE COMMAND (NORAD) is headquartered at the Cheyenne Mountain Air Station in Colorado Springs, Colorado. Originally known as the Continental Air Defense Command, NORAD was set up in the 1950s by the U.S. and Canadian governments to defend North America against military attacks. Using satellites, radar, and other surveillance systems, NORAD monitors U.S. and Canadian airspace for enemy aircraft, missiles, and space vehicles.

Every year on the evening of December 24, NORAD's satellites and radar systems pick up several "unknown objects" in the skies far north of Canada. Two Canadian fighter jets, CF 18 Hornets, are dispatched to verify the objects' identities. What do the jet pilots encounter? Santa Claus and his reindeer!

SANTA INVADES U.S. AIRSPACE?

Does Santa Claus really fly around the world delivering toys to children on Christmas Eve? The U.S. government seems to think so. According to NORAD's Internet Web page (<http://www.noradsanta.org>), the agency has been tracking Santa's yearly flights from the North Pole since 1955.

As the website explains, NORAD uses satellites, ground-based sensors, and radar to track Santa's flight around the world. But because Santa does not file a flight plan with either the U.S. or Canadian government, NORAD classifies him, his sleigh, and his reindeer as "unknown objects."

According to NORAD's Web page, "Two Canadian jets are deployed in the far north of Canada to verify that the objects are, in fact, Santa, Dasher, Dancer, Prancer, Vixen, Comet, Cupid, Donder, Blitzen, and Rudolph. The pilots are still surprised to this day to see a smiling, jolly little man in red waving to them from an open sleigh in the middle of a snowstorm."

CRITICAL DATA

As NORAD follows Santa's path on Christmas Eve, it posts a map of his route on its website. How does Santa make deliveries around the world so fast? According to calculations by NORAD scientists, Santa has perhaps two or three ten-thousandths of a second to deliver toys to each child in the world who believes in him. At that rate, NORAD researchers speculate that perhaps Santa does not tell time the way we do. NORAD states:

> The fact that Santa Claus is more than 15 centuries old and does not appear to age is our biggest clue that he does not work within time as we know it. His Christmas Eve trip may take around 24 hours, but to Santa it could be that it lasts days, weeks, or months. Santa would not want to rush the important job of bringing Christmas happiness to a child, so the only logical conclusion is that Santa somehow functions on a different time and space continuum.

NORAD has calculated some astounding statistics on the popular Christmas gift giver. For instance, NORAD experts figure that Santa eats about four cookies, left for him by the children he visits, per stop. If the average cookie weighs about three-quarters of an ounce, the scientists explain, and if Santa visits roughly 750 million households on Christmas Eve, that's about one ton of cookies every 12,500 households. The total for Santa's worldwide nightly intake: more than seventy-thousand tons! And what about the milk he drinks to wash down all those cookies? That's 375 million pints!

This depiction of Santa Claus wearing a fur suit and cap, boots, and a backpack appeared in a New York weekly newspaper in 1844.

What kind of sleigh does Santa drive? NORAD explains that it is a versatile, all-weather vehicle. It can travel vast distances without refueling and can carry thousands of tons of presents. The sleigh is equipped with the latest navigational equipment—the Global Positioning System.

ONLY KIDDING?

NORAD's Santa Claus website might sound like a lot of fun and silliness, but to millions of young children around the world, Santa is no joke. Santa Claus, and Saint Nicholas before him, has brought joy and excitement—and presents—to children for almost one thousand years. His story goes back even further. It's a fascinating tale of faith, love, and generosity to children. This book tells that story.

The story of Christmas, and Santa Claus, begins with the birth of Jesus Christ, pictured above with Mary and Joseph.

Chapter ONE

THE GIFT OF THE MAGI

THE STORY OF SANTA CLAUS, THE JOLLY FAT MAN with a snowy-white beard and red suit, begins with the story of Christmas itself. That story starts more than two thousand years ago, with a decree by the most powerful man in the Roman Empire, Caesar Augustus. Because running a government required lots of money, Augustus ordered everyone in the empire to pay a new tax. To make sure that nobody was missed, all people living under Roman rule had to be counted. The Roman word for this count was *census*. The census decree demanded that people be counted in the places of their birth.

For a carpenter named Joseph, the order meant a long trip. He lived in the small town of Nazareth, in the ancient kingdom of Palestine (modern-day Israel and Jordan), which was then a Roman province. But Joseph had been born in the town of Bethlehem, far to the south. A law-abiding citizen, Joseph obediently left Nazareth with his wife. Her name was Mary, and she was due to have a baby.

A boy was born soon after the couple arrived in Bethlehem. They named him Jesus. But according to the New Testament of the Bible, his was not an ordinary birth. Miraculous things happened. Angels appeared in the sky and told frightened shepherds that the baby was the long-awaited savior and king of Israel. The Greek name for this savior was Christ.

Another sign of the birth was a star shining above Bethlehem—shining so brightly that it could be seen for hundreds of miles. Far to the east of Bethlehem, three highly educated men saw the star shining. They might have been astrologers, people who studied the heavens and interpreted the arrangement of stars to predict the future. Whoever they were, the three men wondered if the new star was the one that had been mentioned in Jewish prophecies: a sign that a king had been born in Israel. To find out, the men traveled in the direction of the star.

When the three travelers reached the village of Bethlehem, they found a baby in a very unlikely place for a king. He had been born in a stable and was lying on a bed of hay. Because the men had expected to find a king, they'd brought expensive gifts: gold and two

The Magi greet Jesus.

Before the ancient Romans converted to Christianity, they celebrated Saturnalia, a weeklong Roman holiday that ended on December 24.

kinds of precious spices, frankincense and myrrh.

Although the Bible does not say who the three men were, they have been called the Three Kings and the Three Wise Men. They also have been called the Magi, meaning "sorcerers," and by the names Gaspar, Melchior, and Balthasar. Although no one can say for sure who the men were and where they had come from, it's agreed that they had brought with them the first Christmas gifts.

NEW TRADITIONS

Of course, no one at that time thought of Jesus' birthday as Christmas. Nor did people celebrate the day by copying the Magi and giving presents to one another, especially to children. Many centuries would pass before calendars marked December 25 as Christmas Day.

How that date was selected involves another famous Roman leader, Julius Caesar. In 46 B.C., Caesar created a new and more precise calendar, setting new dates for a weeklong holiday dedicated to Saturn, the Roman god of agriculture. In the new calendar, the holiday started on December 17 and ended on December 24. One of the customs of the celebration was giving dolls to children.

The Saturnalia, as the Romans called the holiday, remained on the calendar until a new religion came to Rome—Christianity. Based on the teachings of Jesus, Christianity gradually spread throughout the Mediterranean world. It became Rome's official religion in A.D. 392. The old gods, such as Saturn, were no longer worshiped. The Saturnalia became a celebration of the birth of Christ, observed on December 25.

In Asia Minor (modern-day Turkey), the eastern part of the Roman Empire, Christmas was celebrated not on December 25 but on the day the Three Kings were said to have arrived in Bethlehem—January 6. It was in Asia Minor in the fourth century A.D. that the Magi's gift giving became associated with a bishop named Nicholas, who later became known as Santa Claus.

A painting from the 1500s shows Saint Nicholas distributing nuts to children.

Chapter **TWO**

A SAINT NAMED NICHOLAS

THE STORY OF **N**ICHOLAS, THE MAN WHO WOULD become "Santa Claus," begins seventeen hundred years ago—about three centuries after the Magi brought gifts to Jesus in the stable in Bethlehem. Nicholas lived in Lycia, a region in the western part of modern-day Turkey. Although historians do not know many details about Nicholas's life, one story made him very famous.

The story tells us that Nicholas's parents were Christians. They had been praying for a child for many years before his birth. They were also very wealthy and were able to provide everything that their son needed. But they soon discovered that little Nicholas did not care about toys or playing boys' games. He preferred to spend his time learning, especially about religion.

The story explains that when Nicholas was eight years old, a plague swept through his hometown of Patora and claimed his parents' lives. He inherited all their wealth, including three bars of gold. The death of his parents left Nicholas feeling very lonely. He was also very shy. Rather than looking for friends, he spent a lot of time wandering around the town by himself.

During these walks, Nicholas could not fail to notice that many of the people he passed in the streets were so poor that they had to plead for handouts of food and money. Many of these beggars were children. Nicholas decided to help as many people as he could, but being so shy, he could not bring himself to do so openly. Instead, he would slip a coin into a beggar's hand and move on so quickly that the recipient would not learn Nicholas's identity.

One night as he walked toward his house, Nicholas passed the home of a man who had once been almost as rich as Nicholas's own father. Unfortunately, the man had fallen on hard times. He no longer could provide for himself and his three daughters. As Nicholas came to the house, he saw the family through an open window. Seated around a table that should have been covered with food, the family looked very sad and hungry.

In those days, when a woman got married, it was

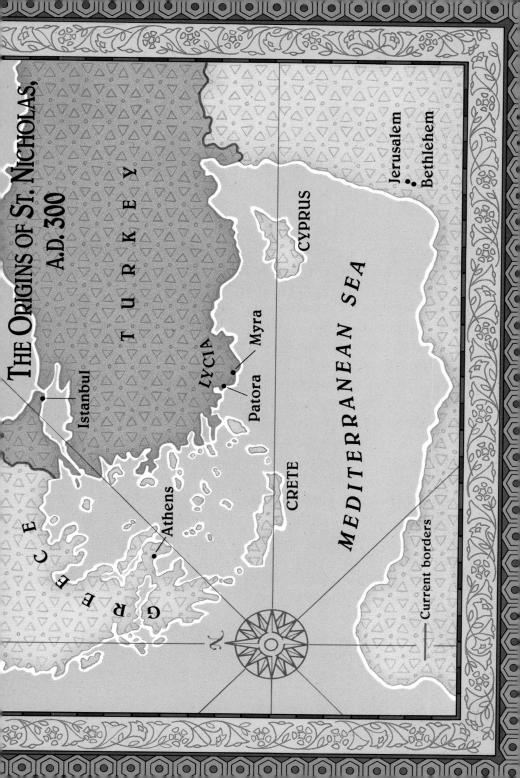

The Origins of St. Nicholas, A.D. 300

TURKEY

Istanbul

LYCIA

Patora

Myra

GREECE

Athens

CRETE

CYPRUS

Jerusalem

Bethlehem

MEDITERRANEAN SEA

Current borders

N

common for her father to give the groom a dowry—a gift of money or property. While Nicholas peered through the window, he heard the man tell his oldest daughter that she could not marry the young man she loved because the father had no dowry to give.

When Nicholas reached home, he could not get their plight out of his mind. The situation seemed so unfair. Here a nice man and his daughters were suffering— while Nicholas had been lucky enough to inherit so much wealth. He thought about the three gold bars he had tucked away in a closet. They'd been there so long, they were covered with dust. What if he gave one to the man?

Nicholas knew enough about the fellow to under- stand that he would be too proud to accept the gift. The man was not likely to beg in the street. The trick of dropping a coin would not work. If Nicholas were to give the man and his daughters a gold bar, he would have to find a way to do it secretly. Then Nicholas remembered the open window. Why not wait until the middle of the night and drop the gold bar through the window when the man and his daughters slept? That's what Nicholas did.

The next night, when Nicholas passed the open win- dow, he heard the man and the girls laughing and happily making plans for the eldest daughter's wed- ding. The story continues to tell how Nicholas gave the man the remaining two bars of gold, so that the other daughters would also have dowries. In another version of the tale, it is not gold bars that Nicholas drops through the open window but sacks of gold, which happen to fall into stockings that had been hung up to dry.

THE LEGEND GROWS

Soon after disposing of the gold, according to legend, young Nicholas decided to devote his entire life to the service of God by becoming a priest. To find inspiration, he left Patora, crossing the Mediterranean Sea for a visit to the holy sites in Israel. Arriving in the city of Jerusalem, he prayed at places that had been important in Jesus' life. During one of Nicholas's prayers, a voice told him to return to Lycia and continue to help the poor. He left immediately.

In those days, a voyage across the Mediterranean Sea was risky business. Pirate raids were a constant danger. But a much more likely threat to safe passage was the weather. A storm could emerge out of nowhere. Nicholas had heard plenty of stories about such tempests from the sailors whose ships docked at Patora. So he was not surprised that a storm arose on his way home.

As sailors worked hard to keep the ship from sinking, the only thing Nicholas could do was kneel on the pitching deck and pray. Minutes after he began, according to legend, the winds dropped and the sea became calm. Once he was safely at home, Nicholas did as the voice had instructed him—he worked among

Saint Nicholas, Bishop of Myra

the poor. As he did, he continued his practice of not calling attention to himself.

Not long after Nicholas's return, the archbishop of Myra died (Myra was a town near Patora). As the priests gathered to pick a successor, one priest told of a dream he'd had. In this dream, God said that the new archbishop would be the first man to enter a certain church on a certain day. To the group's surprise, that man turned out to be the shy young priest known for his work among the poor. When the priests told Nicholas that he was to be their new leader, he was astonished. Because he was so young, people called him the "Boy Bishop."

Although most stories about Nicholas are unsubstantiated, we do know that a bishop named Nicholas lived in Myra. One story holds that because Nicholas preached Christianity, he was imprisoned in A.D. 300 by the Roman emperor Diocletian and that another ruler, Constantine the Great, freed him. His name is recorded among church leaders who attended a conference in the city of Nicaea in A.D. 325. It's believed that Nicholas died a very old man in the year 343 and was buried in Myra. The date of his death has been recorded as December 6.

NICHOLAS AND MIRACLES

After Nicholas died, the stories of his kindness and miraculous deeds grew. It was said that as a newborn baby, Nicholas was able to stand on his own while his

mother bathed him. On days when Christians were expected to fast, the legends said, the infant Nicholas
would not take milk from his mother's breast until
after sundown.

Many stories about Nicholas involve sailors and
storms at sea. According to one legend, a monk
named John called upon Nicholas to save a ship during a terrible storm. Nicholas did so. Another story
tells how Nicholas saved a rich man from drowning
by spreading his coat on the water like a life raft. In
yet another story, an Egyptian man promised to become a Christian if Nicholas saved him from drowning. Nicholas carried the man safely to land. It's no
wonder, then, that Nicholas later became the patron
saint, or protector, of sailors.

One unusual story says that Nicholas stopped at an
inn on his way to the conference at Nicaea. The
owner was a cruel man who had killed three boys,
chopping up their bodies and putting them in barrels
of pickle brine. According to this tale, Nicholas found
the boys, put their bodies back together, and brought
them back to life. This deed amazed the cruel
innkeeper so much that he immediately converted to
Christianity.

Because of the miracle of the three boys, Nicholas
became known as the saint who looks after children.
Children who prayed to Nicholas, it was said, would
have their prayers fulfilled. One early writer declared,
"Happy the city of Myra, to receive such a shepherd

Saint Nicholas became the patron saint of sailors.

Saint Nicholas is said to have brought three dead boys
back to life by putting their dismembered bodies back
together.

The underground church of Saint Nicholas in Bari, Italy

as you, full of love for the children, such a protector."

Even in death, Nicholas was said to work miracles. Five years after he died, for example, a great famine struck Lycia. A relative named Theodulos claimed to see Nicholas's spirit instruct people to gather for prayer at his tomb. As they did so, an earthquake struck, breaking open Nicholas's coffin. Out of it came the sweet aroma of myrrh. Suddenly, despite the famine, no one felt hungry.

The next day, according to the story, five ships filled with grain arrived in the port of Myra. Sailors claimed that a man had appeared to them at sea. He'd walked on the water, bought their grain, and ordered it delivered to Myra. The bakers of Myra then used the grain to make loaves of bread, which were called Saint Nicholas loaves. Because of that deed, Nicholas was also considered the patron saint of bakers.

Some seven hundred years after Nicholas's death,

the Turks conquered Asia Minor, including Lycia. By then, Nicholas was revered among Christians throughout Europe and the Mediterranean world. But because the Turks were Muslims, devout Christians feared that they would no longer be permitted to visit Nicholas's burial place in Myra. They also feared that the Turks would destroy the tomb. In response, a large group of Christians attacked Myra, carrying Nicholas's remains to the town of Bari in Italy. There, the Christians erected a magnificent basilica to house the remains. People who visited the shrine claimed that a strange liquid oozed from Nicholas's casket. When applied to the skin, the liquid was said to heal the sick.

THE CHILDREN'S SAINT

Are the stories of Nicholas and the miracles true? No one can say for sure. But many people believed in the stories and in the saint named Nicholas. In the sixth century A.D., the Roman emperor Justinian built the first church of Saint Nicholas in Constantinople, Turkey. By the year 1500, more than three thousand churches had been built in Nicholas's honor in Germany, France, and Holland. England alone had 446 churches named for Nicholas. Russians named him the patron saint of their country and of the city of Moscow.

For his legendary good deeds, Nicholas had been named the patron saint of both sailors and bakers. According to the original story of Nicholas's generosity,

Church of Saint Nicholas in Prague, Czech Republic

Ruins of Saint Nicholas Church in Turkey

Saint Nicholas became the patron saint of children.

the three gold bars had been exchanged for money at a pawnbroker's shop. Because of this exchange, three gold balls became the symbol of pawn shops, and Nicholas became the pawnbrokers' saint. Because he had provided dowries for the three daughters, he also became the patron saint of marriage. One prayer mentioned "Blessed Nicholas as protector of innocence whilst he lived, and after his death by countless miracles." The prayer asked God to grant people freedom from injustice. Thus, Nicholas also became the patron of the innocent, lawyers, judges, and even prisoners.

But it was as the patron saint of children that Nicholas's fame spread. If children were good, they were told, they would be rewarded with gifts on Saint Nicholas Day—December 6, the date of Nicholas's death. Children only had to hang up a stocking or put out a shoe, and Nicholas would fill it with gifts—but only those stockings and shoes of *good* girls and boys. A twelfth-century children's prayer asked:

> Saint Nicholas, patron of good children,
> I kneel for you to intercede.
> Hear my voice through the clouds
> And this night give me some toys.

NICHOLAS AND HIS ASSISTANT

Throughout Europe, the stories of Nicholas's visits to children became more and more fanciful. In Germany, Belgium, and the Netherlands, Nicholas was said to visit the homes of children on a flying white horse with eight hooves. He would fly over rooftops and peek down chimneys to find out which children were good and which were bad. Because none of the earliest stories about Nicholas contained a reference to a horse, it's believed that the Saint Nicholas story in these northern European countries was influenced by myths about Woden, a pre-Christian, Germanic god said to ride an eight-legged horse.

To be certain that the children had been good, Saint Nicholas was said to have the help of a scary assistant. In Germany and Austria, the assistant was called

In Germany, Knecht (knight) Ruprecht visits children on December 6.

by several names: Knecht Ruprecht, Krampus, and Beelzebub. The French called him Saint Fouettard. In Holland, the helper was named Nicodemus. He was a nasty-looking character who carried a whip and sticks for punishing bad children.

Children in Spain knew the assistant as Black Peter. According to a Spanish tale, Nicholas met Peter when they were both prisoners in Spain. They escaped and then traveled the world, helping people in need and rewarding good girls and boys with gifts. If Black Peter found a bad boy or girl, he would put the child in a burlap sack and carry him or her back to Spain.

Nearly one thousand years after Nicholas's death, he was one of the most beloved religious figures in all of Europe. A thirteenth-century writer explained, "There are holidays that the people observe with special attention. The clerk and the soldier, the tiller of the soil, women, the sailor, the merchant, pay thanks to Nicholas."

Saint Nicholas, dressed as a bishop, visits a Dutch family.

OTHER CHRISTMAS VISITORS

The story of a kindly gift-giving man appealed so much to everyone that Saint Nicholas's Day, December 6, was more important in many countries than Christmas itself. But some people objected to more importance being given to December 6 than to December 25, the day to celebrate Jesus' birthday. One man who objected was a German priest named Martin Luther (1483–1554), founder of the Protestant movement. As

Luther's influence grew in Germany, the holiday tradition there changed. Children no longer received gifts on Saint Nicholas Day. Instead, Christmas was the time for gifts, and the gift giver was said to be the Christ child himself, called Christkindel—later Kris Kringle.

The idea of a Christmas or wintertime visitor—distinct from Saint Nicholas—was an ancient one in Europe. Some such visitors were based on old folktales. Others were based on the story of Jesus Christ. Still other visitors were a combination of folk and religious figures.

In Denmark and Norway, the legendary gift giver was called Julenissen. He was said to be an elf, only a foot tall, with white hair, a long beard, and a pointed red cap. On Christmas Eve, children left him bowls of porridge. As a family slept, Julenissen appeared with a huge sack of presents, which he hid all around the house. One big package, addressed to one family member, had a smaller package inside, addressed to someone else. This package contained a smaller package with a different recipient's name. It held an even smaller package, and so on until the final package was revealed—a very small present for the true recipient.

People in Finland called their Christmas visitor Joulupukki. He arrived from Lapland, a cold region in the far north of Scandinavia, on a sled pulled by a reindeer. Sometimes Joulupukki was accompanied by elves. He was said to be very old, with a long white

Finland's gift-bearing Christmas visitor is named Joulupukki.

mustache, a white cap with blue bands, and a fur-trimmed red coat. He was also known by the names Old Ukko and Great Ukko.

In Poland, Star Man appeared on Christmas Eve, but he didn't come down from the sky. He was usually played by the village priest or another local man and was often accompanied by Star Boys, who sang carols and carried glowing stars. Instead of arriving when children slept, Star Man met with the boys and girls of the village, who answered his questions about religion and prayers. He then gave them gifts that they had asked for in letters to the Mother Star, left on windowsills in the weeks before Christmas.

A small boy in Paris, France, admires a Christmas tree adorned with lit candles.

A NAME FOR THE PEOPLE

n the Greek language, Nicholas means "victor of the people." As Saint Nicholas became more and more popular throughout Europe, many boys and girls were named after him. European versions of this name included Niccolo, Nicola, Nikolai, Niklaas, and Miklos. Other names were shortened versions of Nicholas or variations such as Neil, Nils, Colin, Colette, Cole, Klaas, and Klaus. Many American children are still given the name Nicholas or a variation.

In Russia, Grandfather Frost and the Snow Maiden arrived not on Christmas but on the first day of the new year. They were not religious figures but characters from an old Russian folktale of a woodcutter and his wife who had no children. One day, according to the tale, the couple made a figure out of snow, called the Snow Maiden. She was so beautiful that the woodcutter and his wife called her "daughter." Observing them from the woods, a figure named Grandfather Frost felt sorry for the couple. He used magic to bring the Snow Maiden to life. Unfortunately, when spring came, she melted away. Her spirit was carried into the heavens by Grandfather Frost and another magical figure, Mother Snow. But, to the delight of the children of Russia, the Snow Maiden came back every year with Grandfather Frost to give presents to good children.

Samichlaus, the Christmas gift giver in Switzerland, had a name that sounds very much like Santa Claus. Wearing a bishop's robe, he did not hide from children. Instead he greeted them with questions about their behavior. In case some children had been bad, Samichlaus had a helper named Schmutzli (somewhat like Black Peter), who threatened to punish them.

In Belgium, the Christmas Eve visitors were Noël (Father Christmas) and Christkind (Baby Jesus). Their names were Père Noël and le Petit in France. Italian children looked forward to visits from Babbo Natale (Father Christmas) and Bambino Gesu (Baby Jesus), as well as from la Befana, a kindly old witch who arrived on January 6. The Christmas visitor in Sweden was called Jultomten. Iceland's gift giver was named Jolasveinn.

JUST SAINT NICK

The gift-giving visitor of the Dutch, though, was the same old Saint Nicholas. He made his rounds not on Christmas but on his day—December 6. His name in Dutch was Sinterklaas (*sinter* means "saint"; *klaas* is short for "Nicholas").

Dressed as a bishop, Sinterklaas was tall and thin—

THE ENGLISH CHRISTMAS

No Europeans had more influence on the modern celebration of Christmas than the Celts, the first residents of the British Isles. The Celts and other early British peoples were converted to Christianity by a priest named Augustine of Canterbury. When he arrived in England in 597, he found people practicing the religion of the Druids, ancient Celtic priests.

Just as Christians had turned the Saturnalia, an ancient Roman festival, into a holiday to mark the birth of Jesus, Augustine took portions of the Celtic religion and made them part of the English Christmas. For instance, from the Celtic winter festival of Nolagh, he borrowed the Yule log, holly, and mistletoe. To the Druids, kissing someone under a sprig of mistletoe symbolized the end of grievances. Kissing someone under mistletoe became an English Christmas tradition as well.

Augustine proved so successful as a missionary that on Christmas Day in 598 more than ten thousand English converts were baptized as Christians. By the year 734, Christianity was the official English religion. The birthday of Jesus was celebrated there for twelve days (December 25 to January 6).

For a time, beginning in the mid-1600s, some Christmas traditions were banned in England. The old songs, symbols, and decorations were considered to be unholy pagan rituals. But toward the end of the next century, this attitude began to change. More and more, people in England began restoring old customs. By the time Queen Victoria assumed the throne in 1837, the English were ready to again celebrate Christmas as a joyful time of gaily decorated trees, carol singing, festive dinners, and gift giving. This change was helped along by the popularity of *A Christmas Carol*, Charles Dickens's heartwarming story about Tiny Tim and Ebenezer Scrooge.

However, the English did not return to stories of Saint Nicholas and his visits. Instead, a character named Father Christmas was said to bring gifts to English children at Christmastime.

The burning of the Yule log is an old English Christmas tradition. A huge log was set afire with a torch from the previous year's log. It would burn for awhile each day for twelve days. During the following year, its ashes were used to ward off evil.

and not very jolly looking. When Dutch settlers established a colony in North America in the 1600s, they brought their Sinterklaas with them. In America, he was destined to undergo a dramatic change.

This is how we have come to envision Santa Claus: round as a ball, with a white beard and mustache, a twinkle in his eye, and a sack full of toys.

Chapter THREE

SANTA CROSSES AN OCEAN

THE STORY OF SAINT NICHOLAS FIRST TRAVELED WEST across the Atlantic Ocean with Viking sailors during the eleventh century A.D. They set up a cathedral named for Nicholas in Greenland. When later explorers arrived in the New World, the story of the saint came along. Christopher Columbus, on his first voyage to America, named a harbor for Nicholas in Haiti. The Spanish gave the name Saint Nicholas Ferry to modern-day Jacksonville, Florida.

In the early seventeenth century, English people began to leave their homeland to found colonies in North America. They settled in an area they called New England, where they would be free to practice religion their own way. These settlers—Quakers,

Baptists, Congregationalists, and Presbyterians—recognized December 25 as Christ's birth date, but they chose not to celebrate the day. The New England settlers considered Easter to be the most important holy day for Christians. In Massachusetts, colonists passed a law declaring that "Anybody who is found observing, by abstinence from labor, feasting, or any other way, any such day as Christmas day, shall pay for every such offense five shillings."

HONORING SAINT NICK

To the south of New England, however, in the Dutch colony of New Amsterdam, Christmas was celebrated with enthusiasm. Unlike the English settlers, residents of New Amsterdam considered Christmas a very special time—a time in which to honor their version of Saint Nicholas, Sinterklaas.

In fact, the Dutch declared Nicholas their settlement's patron saint—believed to protect everyone in the town. They built a church like one in Amsterdam, Holland, and named it for him. Because Nicholas was also the patron saint of bakers, his day was celebrated with gifts of ginger cakes and marzipan, candies made with ground almonds. In honor of Nicholas's gifts of gold to the three daughters, the cakes and candies were wrapped in gold paper.

The children of New Amsterdam wore wooden shoes called *klompen*. The night before Saint Nicholas Day, they placed the shoes in a row before the kitchen

New Amsterdam (modern-day New York) in the 1600s

fireplace. The children believed that as they slept, the saint would ride a horse through the sky—all the way from Holland—stop at each house in New Amsterdam, slide down the chimney, and leave gifts in the wooden shoes. If Saint Nicholas heard that a boy or girl had been bad, he might leave a switch, a kind of whip, instead of a present—a warning to the child not to be naughty in the future.

The Dutch ruled New Amsterdam until 1664, when the colony was taken over by the English and renamed New York. Despite the English settlers' disdain for Christmas frivolity, the Dutch of New York held on to their customs—combining Saint Nicholas Day and Christmas into one big celebration. On December 23, 1773, *Rivington's Gazeteer,* a New York newspaper,

Members of a Santa club pose for this photograph.

American writer Washington Irving depicted Santa Claus wearing a Dutch hat and long stockings and smoking a pipe.

noted that "The anniversary of St. Nicholas, otherwise called St. a Claus, was celebrated at Protestant Hall . . . with great joy and festivity."

In the late 1700s, New Yorkers formed a group called the Sons of Saint Nicholas. Its members were descendants of the original Dutch settlers. Soon the city was full of places and organizations honoring Nicholas—its patron saint. Almost all such places were churches, but the city also had a Saint Nicholas Arena (famous for professional boxing matches), the Saint Nicholas Society (founded in 1835), and the St. Nicholas Club (founded in 1875).

The New York Historical Society held its annual meeting on Saint Nicholas Day, December 6. At the meeting in 1809, a member offered this toast: "To the memory of Saint Nicholas. May the virtuous habits and simple manners of our Dutch ancestors be not lost in the luxuries and refinements of the present time." A guest at the dinner was a writer named Washington Irving. He became so interested in the Dutch settlement of New Amsterdam that he published a satirical book called *A History of New York from the Beginning of the World to the End of the Dutch Dynasty,* written by a fictional character named Diedrich Knickerbocker.

Saint Nicholas (Sinterklaas) appeared in Irving's book, but he did not dress in the traditional robes of a bishop. Instead he wore a typical broad-brimmed Dutch hat and long stockings. He puffed a long clay pipe. Sinterklaas did not ride a horse either. He "came riding over the tops of the trees" in a wagon that landed on rooftops. He bounded out, "drawing forth magnificent presents from breeches pockets," and slid down chimneys to leave gifts. Sometimes, if he could not fit down a certain chimney, he dropped the gifts into it.

When Sinterklaas entered a house, he tried not to be seen. But in Irving's story, a man named Van Kortlandt watched him. "And when St. Nicholas had smoked his pipe," Irving wrote, "he twisted it in his hatband, and laying a finger beside his nose, gave the astonished Van Kortlandt a very significant wink, then mounting his wagon, he returned over the treetops and disappeared."

Irving's history, with its tale of a visit from Saint Nicholas, proved very popular. It also sparked imitators. The year after Irving's book appeared, a publication called *The Spectator* published this:

Oh good holy man! Whom we Sancte Claus name,
The Nursery forever your praise shall proclaim:
The day of your joyful revisit returns,
When each little bosom with gratitude burns,
For the gifts which at night you so kindly impart
To the girls of your love, and the boys of your
    heart.

Then holy St. Nicholas! all of the year,
Our books we will love, and our parents
    revere,
From naughty behavior we'll always refrain,
In hopes that you'll come and reward us again.

Several years after Washington Irving's book achieved its success, a British publication, *Gentlemen's Magazine*, took notice of the Dutch New Yorkers' Christmas gift giver. The writer, who obviously did not believe in such things, called the character "Sandy Claus." The writer said that as soon as the little ones went to sleep, their parents filled "a clean stocking near the chimney with all sorts of bon bons, toys, picture-books, etc."

But other writers had no interest in mocking Irving's

story. Indeed, Washington Irving's writings about Saint Nicholas made such an impression on one writer that he took up his pen to compose a poem. It would give Santa Claus a wholly American look.

THE AMERICANIZATION OF SANTA CLAUS

Born in 1779, Clement Clarke Moore was a highly respected author, and biblical student and teacher of Hebrew. In 1822, he lived with his wife and six children in Chelsea, a fairly rural section of Manhattan. We do not know when he read Washington Irving's book with its story about the Dutch Sinterklaas. But there's no doubting Moore did—he was so impressed by the story that, as a Christmas amusement for his children, he wrote a poem about the Christmas visitor:

'Twas the night before Christmas, when all
    through the house
Not a creature was stirring, not even a mouse;
The stockings were hung by the chimney with
    care,
In hopes that St. Nicholas soon would be there;
The children were nestled all snug in their beds,
While visions of sugar plums danced in their
    heads;
And mama in her kerchief, and I in my cap,
Had just settled our brains for a long winter's
    nap—
When out on the lawn there arose such a clatter,

I sprang from my bed to see what was the
  matter.
Away to the window I flew like a flash,
Tore open the shutters and threw up the sash.
The moon, on the breast of the new-fallen snow,
Gave a lustre of midday to objects below;
When what to my wondering eyes should appear,
But a miniature sleigh and eight tiny reindeer,
With a little old driver, so lively and quick
I knew in a moment it must be St. Nick.
More rapid than eagles his coursers they came,
And he whistled and shouted and called them by
  name:

"Now, Dasher! Now, Dancer! Now, Prancer and
  Vixen!
On, Comet! On Cupid! On, Donder and Blitzen!
To the top of the porch, to the top of the wall!
Now, dash away, dash away, dash away all!"
As dry leaves that before the wild hurricane fly,
When they meet with an obstacle, mount to the
  sky,
So, up to the house-top the coursers they flew,
With a sleigh full of toys—and St. Nicholas, too.
And then in a twinkling I heard on the roof
The prancing and pawing of each little hoof,
As I drew in my head and was turning around,
Down the chimney St. Nicholas came with a
  bound.

He was dressed all in fur from his head to his
    foot,
And his clothes were all tarnished with ashes
    and soot;
A bundle of toys he had flung on his back,
And he looked like a pedlar just opening his
    pack,
His eyes how they twinkled! His dimples how
    merry!
His cheeks were like roses, his nose like a
    cherry;
His droll little mouth was drawn up like a bow,
And the beard on his chin was white as the
    snow.
The stump of a pipe he held tight in his teeth,
And the smoke it encircled his head like a
    wreath.

He had a broad face, and a little round belly
That shook, when he laughed, like a bowl full of
    jelly.
He was chubby and plump—a right jolly old
    elf—
And I laughed when I saw him, in spite of
    myself.
A wink of his eye and a twist of his head
Soon gave me to know I had nothing to dread.
He spoke not a word, but went straight to his
    work,

Clement Clarke Moore wrote the famous poem "A Visit from St. Nicholas," later called "'Twas the Night Before Christmas."

And filled all the stockings; then turned with a
  jerk,
And laying a finger aside of his nose,
And giving a nod, up the chimney he rose.
He sprang to his sleigh, to his team gave a
  whistle,
And away they all flew like the down of a thistle;
But I heard him exclaim, ere he drove out of
  sight:
"Happy Christmas to all, and to all a good-night!"

Moore called his poem "A Visit from St. Nicholas."
Because he did not wish to chance ruining his reputa-
tion as a serious writer, he did not allow the poem to
be published. But, the following year (1823), a friend
sent a copy to a friend, who gave the poem to a

newspaper editor in Troy, New York. He published it with this introduction: "We know not to whom we are indebted for the following description of that unwearied patron of Children—that homely but delightful personification of parental kindness—Santa Claus, his costume and equipage, as he hops about visiting firesides of this happy land, laden with Christmas bounties, but from whomsoever it may have come, we give thanks for it."

Over the next ten years, the poem was published twelve times. But it was not until it was printed in the *New York Book of Poetry* in 1837 that Clement Clarke Moore admitted he had written it. A separate children's edition of the poem was published in 1848. Printed along with the poem were seven wood engravings by T. C. Boyd. They were the first sketches of Saint Nicholas published in America.

REINDEER AND A RED SUIT

Moore's poem listed the names of eight reindeer: Dasher, Dancer, Prancer, Vixen, Comet, Cupid, Donder, and Blitzen. Where did Moore get the idea for reindeer? Certainly not from the Dutch. Their Sinterklaas's transportation was provided by a flying horse and wagon. The original Saint Nicholas in northern Europe made his journeys on a white horse. Other Saint Nick stories had him traveling in a cart pulled by a goat or a pair of donkeys. In the story of the Christmas visitor in Finland, the sleigh was drawn by

This undated picture is one of many illustrations that have been drawn over the years to accompany Clement Moore's poem.

This Finnish woman in traditional dress stands with a reindeer.

just one reindeer. It is likely that Moore took the idea of reindeer from another poem by an unknown author. Called *The Children's Friend,* the poem reads in part:

> Old Santeclaus with much delight
> His reindeer drives this frosty night
> O'er chimney-tops, and tracks of snow,
> To bring his yearly gifts to you.

However, Moore was not satisfied with only one reindeer. He gave Santa a team of eight. Moore was a poet. Poems need a rhythm—eight names provided it. Many poems also rhyme, as do Dancer and Prancer and, with a little stretching, Vixen and Blitzen. And

This Italian family admires the display of the Nativity scene (the birth of Jesus).

how much more exciting to have eight reindeer flying through the sky and landing on rooftops than just one. Could a single soaring reindeer send dry leaves whirling upward like a hurricane? Certainly not. But a team of eight? Without a doubt. Santa's use of a sleigh in Moore's poem can be traced to the fact that in New York City in the 1820s, sleighs offered the easiest way to get around on snowy streets.

Another poem by an author whose name we do not

An unknown writer created helpers for busy Santa. He called them "elves."

Thomas Nast's whimsical drawings of Christmas scenes made him famous.

know was published in 1859 in *Harper's Weekly.* Titled
"The Wonders of Santa Claus," it gives a glimpse of
Santa's "little helpers":

> In his house upon the top of the hill,
> And almost out of sight,
> He keeps a great many elves at work,
> All working with all their might,
> To make a million pretty things,
> Cakes, sugar-plums, and toys,
> To fill the stockings, hung up you know
> By the little girls and boys.

Another distinctly American image of the Christmas

Eve caller appeared in a series of drawings in magazines and newspapers between 1860 and 1886. They were made by the most famous cartoonist of nineteenth-century America, Thomas Nast. Born in Germany in 1840, Nast moved to the United States with his family when he was six years old. He studied drawing at the Academy of Design in New York and went to work for *Frank Leslie's Illustrated Newspaper* and then *Harper's Weekly*. He drew his first Santa Claus cartoon in 1860, dressing Santa in a red costume trimmed with white fur and a wide leather belt.

During the Civil War, President Abraham Lincoln asked Nast to draw Santa Claus visiting a camp of Northern soldiers. It is said that when Southern troops saw the drawing, they became very upset to see that Santa was on the side of the North. (After the war, Nast turned to political cartooning. Among his creations were the Democratic donkey and the Republican elephant.)

Together, Washington Irving, Clement Clarke Moore, and Thomas Nast shaped the pattern for all depictions of Santa Claus to this very day. They made the jolly fat fellow with the long white beard and red outfit as American as Uncle Sam. In 1891, President Benjamin Harrison, who had a white beard, dressed up like Santa for his children and read them Moore's poem. Since then, several American presidents have read it to children in the White House, just as millions of parents have done for their children.

Many children believe Santa slides down chimneys to enter their homes.

HOME AT THE NORTH POLE

The poems and tales told much about Santa Claus, but where did he live? An answer came in 1869, when the McLoughlin Brothers published *Santa Claus and His Works.* With drawings by Thomas Nast, the book contained a poem by George P. Webster that not only placed Santa's home at the North Pole but also gave the home a name:

> In a nice little city called Santa Clausville,
> With its houses and church at the foot of the hill
> lives jolly old Santa Claus.

Webster added a toy factory and explained that Santa Claus's residence and workshop could not be seen because they were hidden in snow drifts:

> His home through the long summer months, you
>   must know,
> Is near the North Pole, in the ice and the
>   snow....

In 1885, Thomas Nast also placed Santa's official residence at the North Pole. He sketched two children looking at a map of the route Santa took on his annual journey around the world. In 1890, in a book called *Christmas Drawings for the Human Race,* Nast drew Clement Clarke Moore's Santa and made the round-bellied, white-bearded, jolly old elf appear real

"Dear Santa Claus"

n 1852, residents in a small town in Indiana needed a name for their community. At a meeting held on Christmas Eve, they voted to name their town "Santa Claus." The town got its first post office in 1856, and children's letters to Santa soon began to arrive.

It was not until James Martin became the town's postmaster in 1914 that the letters to Santa were answered, however. Martin answered them himself at first, but soon members of the American Legion pitched in. Eventually, the little post office was receiving four million letters to Santa each year.

Once children learned that Santa Claus lived at the North Pole, many post offices were swamped with mail addressed to, simply, "Santa Claus, North Pole." In 1901, one such letter arrived at a post office in Michigan. It had been sent by the son of car manufacturer Henry Ford. Eight-year-old Edsel Ford asked for a pair of roller skates and a book.

At first post offices did not know what to do with the letters to Santa. They were usually sent to the "dead letter office" and destroyed. But in 1914, John D. Gluck of New York City formed the Santa Claus Association, whose purpose was to distribute letters from poor children to people who could answer the pleas for gifts. The U.S. Postal Service continues to provide such letters to anyone who requests them.

and living. He gave Santa a telescope for checking on kids who were nice and naughty. He also gave Santa a large book for recording children's names.

Another view of Santa's life in the frozen north was provided by the woman who composed the words for

Is there a Mrs. Santa? And does she look like this?

"America the Beautiful." In 1899, Katharine Lee Bates wrote *Goody Santa Claus on a Sleigh Ride,* in which she introduced Mrs. Claus. Taking the Santa story even further in 1908, Bates said that Santa Claus worked so hard on Christmas Eve that he didn't have time to eat a meal. She encouraged children to leave him food. For his hungry reindeer, she proposed that children provide carrots.

SANTA'S LITTLE HELPERS

While Clement Clarke Moore described Santa Claus as a full-grown man, he also called him a "jolly old elf." In Washington Irving's book, from which Moore borrowed a finger beside a nose and a wink, Saint Nick was also called an elf. But a team of elves—Santa's helpers—was the idea of American author Louisa May Alcott, who wrote a short story called "Christmas Elves" in 1856.

Alcott also wrote about Santa for *St. Nicholas Magazine*, which was published yearly from 1873 to 1939. The theme of the magazine was stated in the first issue:

> Hurrah for dear St. Nicholas. He has made friends in a moment. And no wonder. Is he not the boys' and girls' own saint, the special friend of young Americans? Dear old St. Nicholas, with his pet names—Santa Claus, Kriss Kringle, St. Nick, and we don't know how many others.

Each edition included "The St. Nicholas League," a column containing stories sent in by children.

Another description of Santa surrounded by elves was provided in 1902 in a book titled *The Life and*

Adventures of Santa Claus. It was written by one of the most famous authors of children's stories in the world—L. Frank Baum. Baum's first book was *Father Goose.* It proved so successful that he followed it with a tale about a girl in Kansas, a small dog, a tornado, a wicked witch, and a strange land in a faraway place. He titled the book *The Wonderful Wizard of Oz.*

In his Santa Claus book, Baum surrounded Santa with forest creatures, including flying deer called Knooks. Elves known as Ryls and Fairies helped Santa make toys, which were loaded into a huge sack on a sleigh hitched to the Knooks. When it was time to go, Baum wrote, "The deer leaned forward, lifted their slender limbs, and the next moment flew the sledge over the frozen snow." The deer landed on rooftops and waited while Santa slid down chimneys with his bag of gifts.

Santa loved children whether they had been good or bad. Baum wrote: "He knew that the best of children were sometimes naughty, and that the naughty ones were often good. It is the way with children, the world over, and he would not have changed their natures had he possessed the power to do so."

As years and then centuries passed, and the number of children increased all over the world, Baum explained that Santa asked parents to help him with his bigger and bigger yearly task. So what if there were millions and millions more children? "The more the merrier," Santa says with his jolly laugh in Baum's book. "In all the world there is nothing so beautiful as a happy child."

Besides Washington Irving, Clement Clarke Moore, and L. Frank Baum, hundreds of other writers put pen to paper, or used typewriters, to create new stories about Santa. The message of all of them can be found in the last part of "Santa Claus, a Wonder Story for Little Children," in a book by Maud Lindsay. She wrote:

> All the world is happy when Santa Claus comes. Trit-trot, go the little deer, tink, tinkle, ring the bells, O-o-o-o, sing the winds, twinkle, twinkle, shine the stars, and ha! ha! laughs Santa Claus, as he rides over the world to fill the children's stockings, and to bring beautiful gifts.

Children sit on Santa's lap and tell him what they want for Christmas.

Chapter **FOUR**

SANTAS, SANTAS EVERYWHERE

IN THE WEEKS BEFORE CHRISTMAS OF **1841**, A Philadelphia merchant, J. W. Parkinson, had what he called a "crazy idea" to bring customers of German background into his store. He built a fake chimney above the front door and announced that on a certain date, Kris Kringle—the German version of Santa Claus—would come down the chimney before the very eyes of customers. Hundreds of parents showed up with their kids. And, just as promised, Kris popped out of the chimney. Every year after that, Parkinson brought Kris back. A sign in front of the store declared the place to be "Kris Kringle's Headquarters."

Surprisingly, this clever technique was not copied by another merchant for more than fifty years. In 1896, the Boston Store in Brockton, Massachusetts, hired a Scottish immigrant named James Edgar to pretend to be Santa Claus. Edgar proved perfect for the role. He was chubby and had a white beard and a big, booming laugh. When word spread that children could see Santa in person and even talk to him, parents with kids in tow (or was it the other way around?) flocked to the store. Some came by train from Providence, Rhode Island, fifty miles away.

In the next few years, Santas began appearing in department stores, which called their toy departments Santa's Toy Land, Santa's Christmas Wonderland, and other such names. The centerpiece of these displays was Santa seated on a throne. Children were invited to sit on his lap and tell him what they wanted for Christmas. In many stores, children could even have their pictures taken with Santa.

Early in the twentieth century, the biggest department stores in the country's largest cities, such as Macy's in New York and Gimbel Brothers' in Philadelphia, celebrated the arrival of Santa in their toy departments by holding huge parades on Thanksgiving Day. Santa was always the last person to pass by. In Macy's parade, he rode on a float that looked like a huge sleigh. For many years in Gimbel's parade, he rode on the back of a fire engine. When it arrived at the store on Market Street, its ladder was raised, and Santa climbed into the window of the toy department on the sixth floor. Other vehicles that brought Santa

A balloon in the shape of Santa Claus floats over New York City during one of New York's famous Thanksgiving Day parades.

This late nineteenth-century Christmas card shows Santa arriving in a train laden with toys.

to town included trains, airplanes, an autogyro (a combination airplane/helicopter), parachutes, hang gliders, and boats. On at least one occasion, Santa arrived on water skis.

Just how much Santa had become a part of American life was noted on November 27, 1927, by the *New York Times.* An editorial said, "A standardized Santa appears to New York children. Height, weight, stature are almost exactly standardized, as are the red garments, the hood and the white whiskers. The pack full of toys, ruddy cheeks and nose, bushy eyebrows and a jolly, paunchy effect are also inevitable parts of the requisite make-up."

Ideally, the men hired to play Santa would be fat. If

they were not, they were given padding for their red suits—along with fake beards if necessary. Some men who worked as department store Santas year after year grew their own whiskers for authenticity.

By the 1930s, so many men were playing Santa Claus that they formed the National Association of Professional Santas. One of those who delighted in becoming Santa was Dayton C. Fouts, who played the part from 1937 to 1997. When he died at the age of eighty-five, his long run as Santa was listed in *The Guinness Book of World Records.*

Other men dressed as Santa collected money for charities such as the Salvation Army. Occasionally, fathers and uncles put on Santa suits to entertain—or fool—children at Christmastime. Some men made their own Santa Claus suits. Most rented them from costume makers or bought them from department stores. In 1954, the cost of a suit at a Gimbel's store was $24.95. Or a would-be Santa could order a complete outfit by mail from the catalogs of Sears, Roebuck and Co. or Montgomery Ward.

SANTA THE SALESMAN

Through the long history of Saint Nicholas and Santa Claus, some people have frowned upon Christmas gift giving. The New England colonists forbade Christmas festivities, for instance. In modern times, some people disapprove of a holiday in which shopping can seem more important than going to church. They speak out against the commercialization of Christmas. They call Santa Claus a symbol of greed.

But millions of others have found traits in Santa Claus that are not only worthy of praise but also offer valuable lessons for children. Santa works hard. He's kind. He's generous. He treats everyone in the same way. He asks for nothing in return except to request that children are good.

It's no wonder, then, that merchants quickly found Santa Claus to be a very helpful fellow to have in their stores. Once Santa was established in the role of attracting customers, it was but a short and logical step to use him to advertise products.

From Soap to Soft Drinks

One of the earliest manufacturers to use Santa's image commercially was the N. K. Fairbanks Company of Chicago and Saint Louis. It produced Santa Claus Soap. If customers bought enough bars and saved wrappers, they could then trade the wrappers for gifts. The makers of Ivory soap also used Santa Claus to sell products. The company's 1910 Christmas ads showed a little boy leaving a cake of soap with water and a towel, so Santa could wash up after his trip down the chimney.

Before long, ads appeared with Santa as a salesman for almost every kind of product. In the years 1936 to 1938, 20 percent of the Christmas gift ads in *The Saturday Evening Post* and *Ladies' Home Journal* had Santa's picture in them. His image was used to sell

Santa's image is widely used commercially. He is shown here praising Coca-Cola as the soft drink of his choice.

candy, clothes, watches, pipes, cigarettes, cars, and even bananas. With the arrival of television, he appeared in commercials for all sorts of products. The telephone company employed Santa to suggest that a single phone in a home was not enough—he urged people to install phones in their bedrooms, kitchens, and hobby rooms. One of the most famous television ads had Santa sliding down a steep hill—not on his sleigh but on an electric razor. And television manufacturers could not pass up using Santa to sell their latest models.

No company has been more closely connected to Santa Claus than Coca-Cola. Santa first appeared in the firm's advertising in the 1920s. The company told customers, "thirst has no season." Therefore, wintertime was as good as summertime for pausing to enjoy a drink of Coca-Cola. Several artists tried their hand at illustrating Santa for Coca-Cola, but none captured his spirit as well as Haddon Sundblom, one of the country's best illustrators.

Born in 1899 in Muskegon, Michigan, Haddon Sundblom produced ads for breakfast cereals, Maxwell House coffee, several brands of soap, candy, cars, liquor, and even the Marine Corps. He also illustrated stories for major magazines. After going to work for Coca-Cola in 1924, he created pictures that ranged from bathing beauties to soda-fountain scenes.

When asked to create an ad with Santa Claus in it, he decided not to model Santa on the one in Clement Clarke Moore's poem and Thomas Nast's drawings. That Saint Nicholas looked like an elf. Sundblom's Santa would look very much like his friend Lou Prentice! A retired salesman, Lou was tall and had a belly that no one ever described as a little round one. In a 1931 Sundblom painting, shown from the left side and the belt up, Santa's belly is huge. His left hand grasps a whip for driving the team of reindeer. The right hand holds Coca-Cola's unique drinking glass with sloping sides, filled to the brim with the soft drink. The painting was titled *The Pause That Keeps You Going*. (In later years, Sundblom would use himself as the model for Santa.)

Other Sundblom paintings show Santa holding a Coca-Cola bottle. Although it has been opened in the paintings, the contents curiously remain unconsumed. Even in a 1949 ad in which Santa is shown drinking directly from the bottle, it is still full. The ad also features a small boy wearing a Coca-Cola bottle cap like a hat. Introduced in 1942 as "the Sprite Boy," he was used to promote the nickname "Coke."

A Sundblom ad that appeared in 1953 broke with the tradition of Santa paying calls while children slept. It showed him together with a boy and a girl. In a 1959 illustration titled *Refreshing Surprise,* Santa stands at a refrigerator opening a bottle of Coke, while a small boy in pink pajamas watches him. In 1964 he holds a small girl in his lap as she and her little brother admire a dog that is obviously a Christmas gift. These ads represent an interesting change in the Santa story—he becomes almost a member of the family rather than a secret annual visitor. According to Coca-Cola archivist Philip Mooney, Sundblom's interpretations became the definitive American characterization of Santa Claus.

Dudley Moore, left, *and David Huddleston,* right, *star in the* 1985 *film* Santa Claus: The Movie.

Chapter **FIVE**

SANTA OF SONG AND SCREEN

MUSIC HAS ALWAYS BEEN IMPORTANT TO CHRISTMAS celebrations, so it isn't surprising that as Santa Claus became a symbol of the holiday, songs would be written about him. The words of this old song by an unknown composer are typical:

> Jolly old Saint Nicholas.
> Lean your ear this way!
> Don't tell a single soul
> What I'm going to say;
> Christmas Eve is coming soon;
> Now you dear old man,
> Whisper what you'll bring to me;
> Tell me if you can.

When the clock is striking twelve,
When I'm fast asleep,
Down the chimney broad and black,
With your pack you'll creep;
All the stockings you will find
Hanging in a row;
Mine will be the shortest one,
You'll be sure to know.

Johnny wants a pair of skates;
Susy wants a sled;
Nellie wants a picture book;
Yellow, blue and red;

Now I think I'll leave to you
What to give the rest;
Choose for me, dear Santa Claus.
You will know the best.

The first American to tackle Santa in serious music was William Henry Fry. He wrote the "Santa Claus Symphony," first performed in New York City on December 24, 1853. In 1891, J. P. McCaskey published *Christmas in Song, Sketch and Story: Nearly Three Hundred Christmas Songs, Hymns and Carols.* Twenty-three of them were about Santa Claus.

The passage of years brought forth even more tunes. In 1947, the Library of Congress's list of new songs contained twenty-two titles with Santa as the first word. A few songs about Santa, such as "Santa Claus Is Coming to Town," proved so popular that they became as much a part of Christmas festivities as the most familiar religious carols and hymns.

Because Clement Clarke Moore's "A Visit from St. Nicholas" was such a famous poem, it is surprising that no one thought to add music to the words until composer Ken Darby did so more than a century after the poem was written. Darby worked with Fred Waring, leader of The Pennsylvanians, a famous orchestra and chorus of the 1940s and 1950s. When The Pennsylvanians recorded the Moore poem put to music, they used the title "'Twas the Night Before Christmas." It immediately became the most-requested song whenever the group performed, even when it wasn't Christmastime.

In a hilarious Christmas song, singer Eartha Kitt asks Santa for a fur coat and a Cadillac.

Perry Como sang Christmas songs such as "Santa Claus Is Coming to Town" in the 1940s.

Some Santa songs were novelty numbers intended to be humorous. Perhaps the most famous of these was written in the 1940s in the form of a letter from a desperate child whose urgent plea was the song's title: "All I Want for Christmas Is My Two Front Teeth." In a big hit in the 1950s, the very grown-up singer Eartha Kitt teasingly asked "Santa Baby" for a sable fur coat and a Cadillac. Another record told of a child who stayed awake on Christmas Eve in the hope of spotting the jolly old elf. What he saw was his father, disguised in a Santa suit, and what happened next left him confused. "I Saw Mommy Kissing Santa Claus" was the song's title.

The most durable of the popular Santa songs was written by the team of J. Fred Coots and Haven Gillespie and was recorded in the 1940s by singer Perry Como. "Santa Claus Is Coming to Town" advised children that they'd better not cry, pout, or shout, because Santa was checking his lists of those who had been naughty and those who had been nice. "Here Comes Santa Claus," recorded by Gene Autry, "the Singing Cowboy" of the movies, offered a happier picture of Santa and his reindeer coming down Santa Claus Lane with a bag full of toys.

In 1939, a Montgomery Ward store in Chicago added a new figure to the Santa Claus tale—and a new song. A story written by the head of the firm's advertising department, Robert L. May, was given free to customers. It told of Rudolph, a reindeer whose nose was so shiny that other reindeer made fun of him. But one night, when the fog was so thick that everyone at the North Pole feared that Santa would not be able to make his rounds, Santa asked Rudolph to guide his sleigh with the light from his nose.

Three years later, Rudolph, the ninth of Santa's flying reindeer became the star of a movie cartoon based on the story. But he became truly famous when Gene Autry recorded "Rudolph the Red-Nosed Reindeer," with new words written by Johnny Marks. Released for Christmas in 1949, the record sold 2 million copies, and more than four hundred versions of the song were recorded in the next fifty years.

ON-SCREEN SANTA

There is no counting how many times Santa Claus has appeared in movies and on television. The first film in which he was the main character was made in 1903. A short, silent movie in black and white, it showed everything that people had come to expect of Santa: the beard, the costume, the reindeer, the house at the icy North Pole, the workshop, the toys, and a very long telescope for spotting which children had been naughty and nice.

The next important movie about Santa was 1934's *Babes in Toyland*. It was a musical based on an operetta by Victor Herbert and starred comedians Stan

Oliver Hardy, left, *and Stan Laurel,* center, *play elves in the movie* Babes in Toyland.

A scene from the movie Santa Claus Conquers the Martians

Laurel and Oliver Hardy, who played elves working in Santa's toy factory. One of the movie's most famous songs is "The March of the Wooden Soldiers." The film was later re-released under that title. It was also remade twice. The cast of a 1961 version included teenage singing stars Tommy Sands and Annette Funicello. A 1986 remake starred Drew Barrymore and Keanu Reeves. In the opinions of film critics such as Leonard Maltin, neither the 1961 nor the 1986 version is as good as the original Laurel and Hardy movie.

The silliest Santa movie came out in 1964. In *Santa Claus Conquers the Martians,* the jolly old elf and two earth children are carried off to the Red Planet to help solve problems, such as Martian kids watching too much television. Very few people went to see the movie. Those who did couldn't stop laughing at such

Tim Allen stars in the 1994 movie The Santa Clause.

nonsense. The same year, Hollywood released the animated big-screen version of *Rudolph the Red-Nosed Reindeer*, which was a huge success.

The year 1966 brought the Italian-made *The Christmas That Almost Wasn't*, a film that involved the hijacking of Santa. The movie was intended for children, but not many liked it. A Santa Claus movie that opened in 1984 also turned out to be a huge flop. Called *Silent Night, Deadly Night*, it was a gory horror flick in which somebody dressed like Santa Claus goes around killing people. The film made many people angry. It was picketed in many cities and was withdrawn from theaters in less than two weeks.

Faring better the next year (1985) was *Santa Claus: The Movie*, starring Dudley Moore and John Lithgow.

It told the story of how Santa came to be and contained excellent scenes of Santa's workshop and all the other features that you'd expect to find at the North Pole, from the reindeer to Santa's sleigh. A comic actor best known from television, Tim Allen starred in 1994's *The Santa Clause.* He played a man who learns the spirit of Christmas by turning into Santa himself.

How often Santa has appeared on television is impossible to know. Each year he appears in televised Thanksgiving Day parades, situation comedies, variety shows, and even police and detective programs. Santa usually takes part in the annual telecast lighting of the national Christmas tree by the president. For a few years, the jolly person in the beard and red-and-white suit at the lighting was NBC-TV weatherman Willard Scott. Santa has also been played by another jolly weatherman, Al Roker.

Cartoon Santas are especially popular. Easily the most famous Santa cartoon was *How the Grinch Stole Christmas,* based on a story by Dr. Seuss. In the cartoon, the voice of the Grinch, in all his nastiness, was provided by Boris Karloff, the man who played the monster in the movie *Frankenstein.* The show was broadcast shortly before Karloff died in 1969 and is repeated every year. It's possible that more people have seen the Grinch than ever saw Karloff's Frankenstein monster.

Most television critics agree that one of the finest

shows on the subject of Santa was *A Christmas Story,* which first aired in 1983. Based on an episode in the boyhood of radio personality Jean Shepherd, the show features a boy named Ralphie, growing up in the 1940s. Ralphie's Christmas wish is that Santa will bring him a Red Ryder BB gun. The show proved so popular (and realistic) that it has become a staple of television's Christmas-season programming.

The most famous of all Santa Claus movies came out in 1947 and has been shown on television almost every year since the 1950s. Filmed in black-and-white and colorized for television in the 1980s, *Miracle on 34th Street* is about a man who calls himself Kris

Ralphie visits Santa Claus in the 1983 film A Christmas Story.

The 1947 movie Miracle on 34th Street *starring Maureen O'Hara,* left, *Edmund Gwenn as Kris Kringle,* right, *and Natalie Wood,* front, *has become a Christmas classic.*

Kringle and claims to be the real Santa Claus. After he is hired to play Santa in Macy's department store in New York, an official of the store fears that Kris is mentally unbalanced.

Eight-year-old Susie, the daughter of the woman who hired Kris, doubts Kris's claim that he is Santa. When the matter winds up in a state court, the district attorney poses a question to the judge that has been asked for as long as Santa Claus has been around: "Is there or is there not a Santa Claus?"

Famous Arctic and Antarctic explorer, and father of three curious children, Richard E. Byrd planned to check out Santa's hometown by flying to the North Pole in 1926.

Chapter **SIX**

THE BIG
QUESTION

IN **MIRACLE ON 34TH STREET, THE DISTRICT ATTORNEY'S**
question—"Is there or is there not a Santa Claus?"—is
answered by the United States Post Office. When a
worker in New York's main post office finds a letter
that Susie has sent to Kris Kringle at the courthouse,
he remembers the sacks of mail addressed to Santa
Claus that are cluttering up the dead letter office. See-
ing a way to get rid of them, he arranges for Santa's
mail to be delivered to Kris at the court.

Speaking from behind a huge pile of letters that
have been dumped on his bench, the judge declares,
"Since the United States government declares this
man to be Santa Claus, this court will not dispute it.
Case dismissed."

Searching for Santa

In every child's life, there comes a time when the BIG question must be put to a parent: Is there a Santa Claus? One parent who heard the question was Richard E. Byrd, a famous Arctic and Antarctic explorer. Along with pilot Floyd Bennett, Byrd planned to fly over the North Pole in April 1926.

In the 1920s, flying airplanes was not easy or commonplace. Although Bennett was a famous aviation pioneer, no one had ever made such a long and hazardous flight before. No one had ever flown to the North Pole.

Planning for the journey had gone on for many months. "To all the world at large it was all a secret," Byrd wrote. "Only a trusted few were in my confidence." He had told his three children: three-year-old Katharine, four-year-old Bolling, and six-year-old Dickie. On Christmas Eve, the children had come to him with a question that, Byrd wrote, "was delivered with the savage directness of a dagger thrust."

They asked, "Will you see Santa Claus?" Byrd did not answer until Christmas Day. "No, I shan't see Santa Claus," he said, "but when I get back I'll tell you about his place at the North Pole."

Dickie found the reply disturbing. With a frown, he asked, "But there is a Santa Claus, Daddy, isn't there?"

Byrd blurted, "Of course there is a Santa Claus."

In giving that answer, Byrd created a problem for himself. He later wrote, "I had baldly and without

Byrd is dressed warmly for the trip to the North Pole.

reservation told my three babies something about which I myself was not sure. I had told them there was a Santa Claus. How did I know? I had never seen him. But perhaps in the course of the great adventure

I should find that after all Santa Claus does exist."

Byrd traveled by boat to Spitsbergen, Norway, where he boarded a small airplane for his trip. As the craft winged north, Bennett sat at the wheel, and Byrd consulted the compass and other instruments on which their lives depended. Looking out a window, they saw icebergs dotting the cold sea. Soon they found themselves alone in a strange world of blue sky above and white ice beneath. There was nothing else to be seen. Not a living thing—no birds in the air, no bears on the ice. Not a strip of green land. A dead, dead world.

As the plane continued north, Byrd thought about the assurances that he'd made to his three small children. At Christmastime, the ice field he was flying over would be shrouded in darkness. How could anyone make a home in such a place? How strange it seemed that a huge, empty portion of the earth's surface should once a year become so important! Now that he was approaching the North Pole, Byrd asked himself the ageless question: "Is there a Santa Claus?"

Then came the great moment. Byrd and Bennett had reached the North Pole. Below was nothing but ice. It spread clear to the horizon all around. Icebergs were everywhere. Drifted snow formed ridges that zigzagged across the frozen white surface. Was this really the home of Santa Claus? Was this the spot where he kept the record book of good and bad deeds?

As Byrd looked across the bleak scenery and wondered if there was a Santa Claus, one of the plane's three engines started to sputter. It was leaking oil! Byrd wondered if the remaining two motors could keep the plane aloft. To make matters worse, he dropped a navigational tool called a sextant, breaking it beyond repair.

Disappointed and worried about their safety, the men decided to turn back. But, with the sextant broken, they had no way of knowing if strong winds had blown them off course. And if the oil leak forced them to set the plane on the ice, they would have no way of knowing exactly where they were. The plane would certainly be wrecked. The nearest populated area was Greenland, hundreds and hundreds of miles away. And everyone knew that nobody lived at the North Pole!

As Bennett struggled to keep the plane in the air, Byrd again thought about his children. They believed in Santa because their daddy had told them that Santa was real. If their daddy did not come back to them, they would know that he had gone to the land of Santa Claus and never returned! The very thought made Byrd shudder.

Time passed. But the little plane remained airborne. It seemed miraculous—as if it was being held up by an unseen hand. After hours of anxiety and peering through the window, Byrd saw what appeared to be a cloud. But it wasn't—it was land. They were saved! He would see his children again.

But what would he tell them? He had been to the North Pole, and he'd found nothing to indicate that

Santa Claus exists. Or *had* he? Something had kept the crippled plane in the air after all. Something—or someone—had guided it out of danger to a safe landing.

"There is a Santa Claus," Byrd told his children (and wrote in an article about his historic trip, "Santa Claus and the North Pole"). "I know it, for I have been to the North Pole and seen!"

"If You See It in the *Sun*. . . . "

Twenty-nine years before Richard E. Byrd's kids put him on the spot by questioning the existence of Santa Claus, a man named Thomas O'Hanlon of New York City found himself in that very same predicament. In September 1897, he was reading his favorite newspaper, the *New York Sun*. But it was not just another paper. The *Sun* had been publishing news since 1833. Some of its reporters, including Edgar Allan Poe and Horatio Alger, had gone on to become very famous writers.

Not a day went by without O'Hanlon buying a copy of the *Sun*. But as he was reading it on that September day, he was interrupted by his daughter, Virginia. She was very upset about something. O'Hanlon listened as Virginia explained the problem—one the father had been expecting the eight-year-old girl to bring up sooner or later. She asked him, "Is there a Santa Claus?"

O'Hanlon's answer resulted in the most famous letter ever sent to a newspaper:

Dear Editor—I am 8 years old.

Some of my little friends say there is no Santa
  Claus.

Papa says "If you see it in *The Sun* it's so."

Please tell me the truth, is there a Santa Claus?

When the letter arrived at the desk of the paper's editor, Francis P. Church, he replied with the most
reprinted editorial in history:

VIRGINIA, your little friends are wrong. They
have been affected by the skepticism of a skepti-
cal age. They do not believe except what they see.
They think that nothing can be which is not com-
prehensible by their little minds. All minds, VIR-
GINIA, whether they be men's or children's are
little. In this great universe of ours man is a mere
insect, an ant, in his intellect, as compared to the
boundless world about him, as measured by the
intelligence capable of grasping the whole of
truth and knowledge.

Yes, VIRGINIA, there is a SANTA CLAUS. He
exists as certainly as love and generosity and de-
votion exist, and you know that they abound and
give to your life its highest beauty and joy. Alas!
How dreary would be the world if there were no
SANTA CLAUS! It would be as dreary as if there
were no Virginias. There would be no childlike
faith then, no poetry, no romance to make

tolerable this existence. We should have no enjoy-
ment, except in sense and sight. The eternal light
with which childhood fills the world would be ex-
tinguished.

Not believe in SANTA CLAUS! You might as
well not believe in fairies! You might get your
papa to hire men to watch all the chimneys on
Christmas Eve to catch SANTA CLAUS, but even
if they did not see SANTA CLAUS coming down,
what would that prove? Nobody sees SANTA
CLAUS. The most real things in the world are
those that neither children nor men can see. Did

Virginia O'Hanlon, shown here in 1967, always remembered Francis Church's response to her letter asking if Santa Claus really exists.

you ever see fairies dancing on the lawn? Of course not, but that's no proof that they are not there. Nobody can ever conceive or imagine all the wonders there are unseen and unseeable in the world.

You tear apart the baby's rattle and see what makes the noise inside, but there is a veil covering the unseen world which not the strongest man, nor even the united strength of all the strongest men that ever lived, could tear apart.

Only faith, fancy, poetry, love, romance can push aside that curtain and view and picture the supernatural beauty and glory beyond. Is it all real? Ah, VIRGINIA, in all this world there is nothing else real and abiding.

No SANTA CLAUS! Thank God! he lives, and he lives forever. A thousand years from now, VIRGINIA, nay, ten times ten thousand years from now, he will continue to make glad the heart of childhood.

This thoroughly modern Santa Claus receives his Christmas lists via the Internet and his laptop computer.

EPILOGUE

WHAT LIES AHEAD FOR SANTA CLAUS? SINCE Santa is a timeless figure, he should have no problem keeping up with the high-tech changes of the twenty-first century. To be sure, Santa has always tried to stay in step with mass communication. For example, not long after the telephone was invented in the late nineteenth century, one of Thomas Nast's drawings showed Santa using a phone to listen to a child request a gift. Over the years, Santa has sent his message of goodwill to children via television, radio, and the movies.

At the beginning of the twenty-first century, Santa uses a computer. Instead of writing letters to Santa, children can send him requests by e-mail. Many

Internet websites are devoted to Santa Claus. Just search for the keyword *Santa* on your Web browser, and you'll find them.

One site, <http://www.mofile.fi/santa/port/sanfaq.htm>, provides a list of frequently asked questions about Santa, and the answers. A Santa home page is maintained by Santa, Inc., in Iceland (<http://www.santa.is>). At <http://www.santa-claus.com>, you'll find Christmas recipes, games, electronic Christmas cards, a coloring book, and Santa's Little Helpers Gallery. At <http://www.santaclaus.com>, you'll find lists of books about Santa and the elves and other information, including a count of how many weeks, days, and hours remain before Santa climbs into his sleigh for another trip around the world.

NORAD's website (<http://www.noradsanta.org>) offers the latest in high-track surveillance of Santa Claus as he flies across the sky on Christmas Eve. How rapidly does Santa travel? "Faster than starlight," the website explains. What is his climbing speed? "In the twinkle of an eye."

SOURCES

8   <http://www.noradsanta.org>, n.d.

9   Ibid.

29   Charles W. Jones, *Saint Nicholas of Myra, Bari and Manhattan: Biography of a Legend* (Chicago: University of Chicago Press, 1978), 44.

33   Ibid., 46.

34   Ibid., 60.

35   Ibid., 72.

46   Penne L. Restad, *Christmas in America* (New York: Oxford University Press, 1995), 80.

49   Jones, 333.

50   Ibid., 334.

50   Washington Irving, *Diedric: A History of New York from the Beginning of the World to the End of the Dutch Dynasty* (Philadelphia: Carey Lea & Blanchard, 1838), 52.

51   *The Spectator,* December 1, 1812, 4.

51   *Gentlemen's Magazine,* November 12, 1812, 3.

56   Restad, 10.

58   Ibid.

61   Ibid.

64   Irene Smith, *The Santa Claus Book* (New York: Franklin Watts, 1948), 53.

67   Restad, 95.

68   L. Frank Baum, *The Life and Adventures of Santa Claus* (Indianapolis: Bowen-Merrill, 1902), 80.

69   Smith, 37.

74   Editorial, *New York Times,* November 27, 1927, n.p.

79   Coca-Cola Company, Atlanta, 1992.

82   Restad, 37.

98   Richard Evelyn Bird, *Santa Claus at the North Pole,* quoted in *The Santa Claus Book,* Irene Smith (New York: Franklin Watts, 1948), 184.

BIBLIOGRAPHY

Baum, L. Frank. *The Life and Adventures of Santa Claus.* Indianapolis: Bowen-Merrill, 1902.

Bradford, Roark. *How Come Christmas: A Modern Morality.* New York: Harper & Brothers, 1948.

Brown, Joan Winmill. *Christmas Joys.* Garden City, NY: Doubleday & Company, Inc., 1982.

Church, Francis P. *Yes, Virginia, There Is a Santa Claus.* New York: Delacorte Press, 1992.

Clements, Linda. *The Spirit of Christmas Past: Evocative Memories of Years Gone By.* New York: Smithmark, 1996.

Giblin, James C. *The Truth about Santa Claus.* New York: Thomas Crowell, 1985.

Hadfield, Miles, and John Hadfield. *The Twelve Days of Christmas.* London: Cassell, 1961.

Jones, Charles W. *Saint Nicholas of Myra, Bari, and Manhattan: Biography of a Legend.* Chicago: University of Chicago Press, 1978.

Lane, Julie. *The Life and Legends of Santa Claus.* Harleysville, PA: Tonnis Productions, Inc., 1983.

Lankford, Mary D. *Christmas around the World.* New York: Morrow, 1995.

Paton, Kathleen. *Santa.* New York: Smithmark Publishers, 1998.

Restad, Penne L. *Christmas in America: A History.* New York: Oxford University Press, 1995.

Sansom, William. *A Book of Christmas.* New York: McGraw-Hill Book Co., 1968.

Santas: 4,000 Years of History. Fullerton, CA: M. E. Duncan Co., Inc., 1991.

Smith, Irene. *The Santa Claus Book.* New York: Franklin Watts, Inc., 1948.

Smith, Lissa, and Dick Smith. *Christmas Collectibles: A Guide to Selecting, Collecting and Enjoying the Treasures of Christmas Past.* London: Quintet Books, 1993.

Synder, Phillip. *December 25th: The Joy of Christmas Past.* New York: Dodd, Mead & Company, 1985.

Taylor, J. R., and Barbara F. Charles. *Dream of Santa: Haddon Sundblom's Vision*. Washington, D.C.: Staples & Charles, Ltd., 1992.

FOR FURTHER READING

Hundreds and hundreds of books have been written about Santa Claus. Most have been made up for the entertainment of children. The following deal at length with how Saint Nicholas came to be Santa Claus and how Santa's image has changed:

Paton, Kathleen. *Santa*. New York: Smithmark Publishers, 1998.

Restad, Penne L. *Christmas in America*. New York: Oxford University Press, 1995.

Santas: 4,000 Years of History. Fullerton, CA: M. E. Duncan Co., Inc., 1991.

INDEX

OTHER TITLES FROM LERNER AND A&E®:

Arthur Ashe
Bill Gates
Bruce Lee
Carl Sagan
Chief Crazy Horse
Christopher Reeve
Eleanor Roosevelt
George Lucas
Gloria Estefan
Jack London
Jacques Cousteau
Jesse Owens
Jesse Ventura
John Glenn
Legends of Dracula

Louisa May Alcott
Madeleine Albright
Maya Angelou
Mohandas Gandhi
Mother Teresa
Nelson Mandela
Princess Diana
Queen Cleopatra
Queen Latifah
Rosie O'Donnell
Saint Joan of Arc
Wilma Rudolph
Women in Space
Women of the Wild West

ABOUT THE AUTHOR

H. Paul Jeffers has published forty books of fiction and nonfiction. They include three on President Theodore Roosevelt, a biography of President Grover Cleveland, two on cases of the FBI, and a history of Great Britain's famed police force, Scotland Yard. A former broadcast journalist, he lives and writes in New York City.

PHOTO ACKNOWLEDGMENTS

The images in this book are used with the permission of: © CORBIS, pp. 2, 77, 92; © The Granger Collection, New York, p. 6; © Bettmann/CORBIS, pp. 10, 16, 18, 35, 36, 43, 44, 47, 48, 57; © Mary Evans Picture Library, pp. 12, 28, 74; © Brown Brothers, pp. 15, 49, 55, 59, 61, 95; © Manche/Mary Evans Picture Library, p. 24; © Erich Lessing/Art Resource, NY, pp. 27, 33; © Archive Photos, pp. 29, 63, 84, 91; © Wolfgang Kaehler/CORBIS, p. 31; © Penny Tweedie/CORBIS, p. 32; © The National Board of Antiquities, Finland, p. 38; © Limot/Archive Photos, p. 39; © Robert Fried/Robert Fried Photography, p. 58; © Underwood & Underwood/CORBIS, p. 60; © Harrison Fisher in 'American Girls in Miniature'/Mary Evans Picture Library, p. 66; © Archive Photos/Camerique, p. 70; © La Domenica del Corriere/Walter Molino/Mary Evans Picture Library, p. 73; © Photofest, pp. 80, 88; © Sidamon-Erstoff, Morrison, Warren, Ecker, and Schwartz, p. 83; © Orion/American Stock/Archive Photos, p. 86; © Embassy Pictures/Archive Photos, p. 87; © Archive Photos/Peter Billingsley, p. 90; © CORBIS/BETTMANN-UPI, p. 100; © Donna Day/Tony Stone Images, p. 102.

Front and back covers: © Bettmann/CORBIS.